T0197389

Suzie Q
Fights Leukemia

by Suzie Q

To order additional copies of this book, contact:
Xlibris
844-714-8691
www.Xlibris.com
Orders@Xlibris.com

ISBN: Softcover   978-1-6641-0931-5
          EBook   978-1-6641-0930-8

Print information available on the last page

Rev. date: 10/06/2021

Illustrated by Dr. Sue's granddaughter, Penny Myrowitz, age 9 and cousin Dawna Sandler.

Once upon a time,
a long long time ago,
far far away,
in a land called C-A
there lived Loo
and a little girl named Suzie Q

And she was a happy little girl,
who loved to sing and dance and twirl
but when she met Loo,
all she could say was boo-hoo.

The Land
of
C-A (cancer)

Loo was short for leukemia
acute lymphoblastic leukemia
in the land of C-A
and you might say OK

that's not so bad
but really is sad...

cuz C-A are letters that start the word cake
for words like candy and cupcake
so those words with C-A sound yummy
and are fun for your tummy.

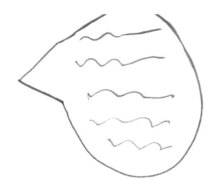

And some might say, that it's important to pray.
To ask G-d to make Loo go away.

Suzie Q is really me,
The story is quite long, you see.
cuz Suzie Q was a busy girl
who loved to sing and dance and twirl

Sorry, I can't come out to play the reason is worse than a rainy day I'm very sorry because I'm sick having Loo is not something I would ~~____~~ pick

She loved to play with her friends,

and messages she would send
To say, "sorry, I can't come out to play
The reason is worse than a rainy day
I'm very sorry because I'm sick
Having Loo is not something I would pick."

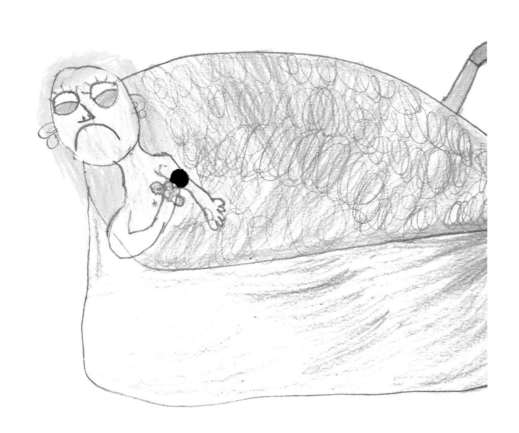

"I really did not have a clue
That Loo is like a bad boo-boo
all over you,
in your body, in your blood,
you can't wash it out, even if you scrub."

There are a lot of kids who have been there, and all the doctors and nurses really care.
Loo didn't only happen to me
Or one kid, or two or even three.
Loo badly affects a lot of us
But the doctors and nurses make a fuss
And give us care and lots of hydration

But let me give you an explanation.

When you are first born and are brand new
300 bones are inside of you
Down to 206 they go.
The middle of each bone has a tube that's narrow
The stuff inside is called "bone marrow."

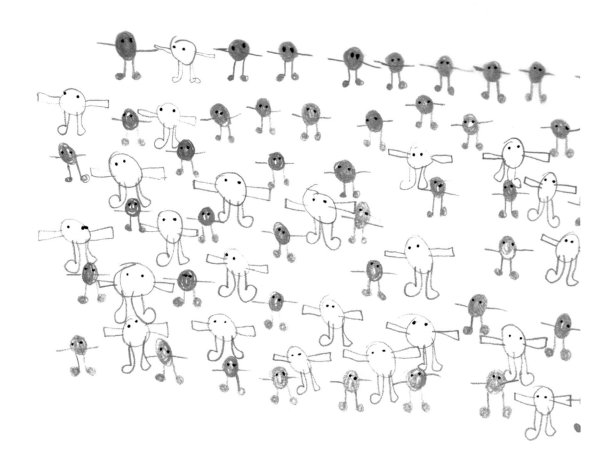

All the bad stuff happens in the bone marrow

Inside the bones, in tubes so narrow.

The red blod cells carry the oxygen,

The platelets "stop the bleed!"

The white blood cells fight the infection

White blood cells, "Lead, Lead, Lead!"

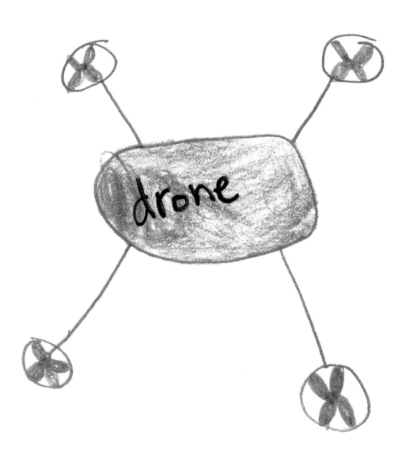

We cannot see what's inside these bones
Maybe we could use little drones

When Suzie Q was having a bad day,
She would sit up in her hospital bed and say,
"Leukemia cells, Leukemia cells,
What are you doing? They would answer her,
We are like coffee, just cooking and brewing."

And Suzie Q would call out again,

"Leukemia cells Leukemia cells,

What are you doing?"

And they would answer, "we are growing and stewing!"

"Leukemia cells, Leukemia cells, What are you doing?

We are canoeing, reviewing, undoing and spewing

We are using, and moving and misconstruing your cells ."

And now your doctors hear the Alarm bells

Red blood cells, white blood cells and platelets too
Combine together to form the goo
That's called "bone marrow" inside the bones,

And usually things are good at home.

Now back to the story of Suzie Q

Whose bone marrow was infected by Loo.

This is true, it's not a rumor

The white cells merged and caused a tumor.

Because of this bad, bad behavior

Suzie Q needed the doctors to save her.

To the hospital she was taken

Hoping the diagnosis was mistaken.

Tests were ordered for Suzie Q to take
CT scans and PET scans, to find where it ached.

They wanted her to have an MRI too,

It's a test with a machine that you have to go through

You lie very still, like when you are in bed.

And slide in a machine from your toes to your head.

It sees inside of your bones and your skin,

And makes pictures to show your doctors where to begin.

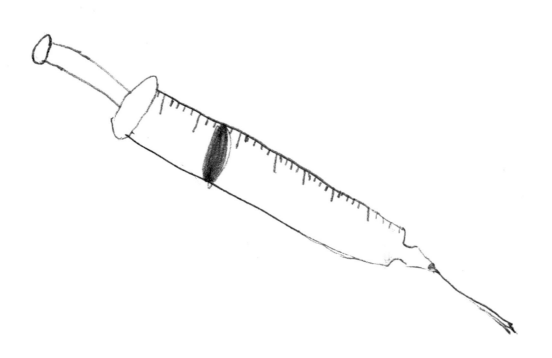

The hospital Nurses give you medicine,
They first make a port, then they will stick in a pin
The port stays there ready for taking blood draws
Though getting a needle makes me want to pause...

Suzie Q has a doctor named Dr. Niyongere
Who said, " it's so important to look cute with what you wear."

So Suzie Q has dresses in blues, purples and reds
So she can feel and look her best when she takes her meds.

Suzie Q was told that she needed a treatment-
Chemotherapy was what she would get.
Suzie Q keeps a smile on her beautiful face
with all this chemo she has to keep up her pace.

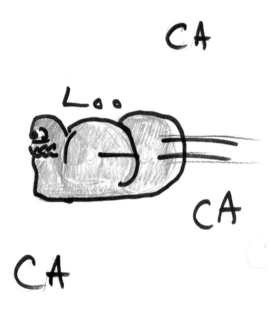

As Suzie Q gets better, she notices things,
Like her fingers swell and she can't wear her rings.

She learned that the chemo caused a lot of conditions,
That didn't quite go with the drugs' healing mission.

your hair might fall out
and you might wanna shout
but your hair will grow back
and your life will get on track

you will start to feel stronger
even if the chemo lasts longer
Eventually you can be good as new
in everything you want to do

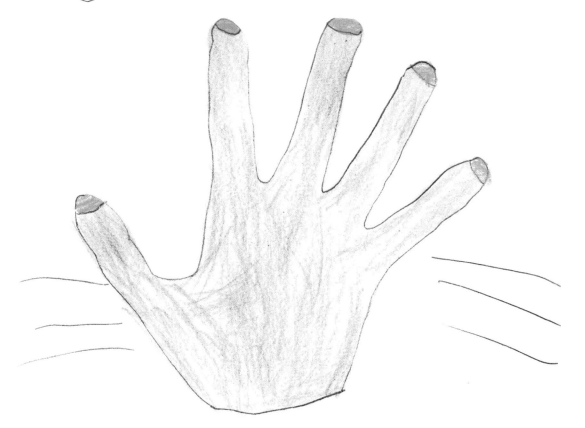

and say good-bye to Loo

Good-bye Loo, Tootle loo, See ya later, alligator

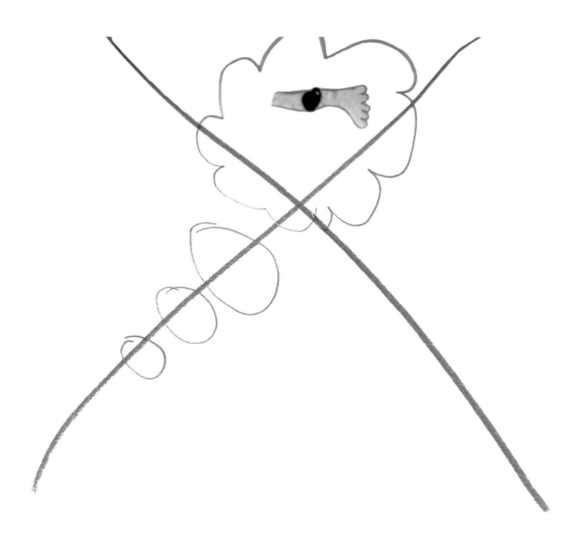

I wanna say good-bye to my leukemia
And I hope to not even have dreams about ya
Please leave my body alone,
And don't call me on my phone

I wanna play with my friends,
And have my regular life again.
Thank you Dr. Niyongere, Marie and Jen
Please keep me well so we don't do this again.

The End.

Be well everyone, Suzie Q
5/10/2020 and revised 9/26/2021

Printed in the United States
by Baker & Taylor Publisher Services